"Each second we live is a new and unique moment of the universe, a moment that will never be again... And what do we teach our children? We teach them that two and two make four and that Paris is the capital of France.

When will we also teach them: do you know who you are? You are a marvel. You are unique. In all the years that have passed, there has never been another child like you. And look at your body – what a wonder it is! Your legs, your arms, your clever fingers, the way you move. You may become a Shakespeare, a Michelangelo, a Beethoven. You have the capacity for anything. Yes, you are a marvel. And when you grow up, can you then harm another who is, like you, a marvel? You must cherish one another. You must work – we must all work – to make this world worthy of its children."

Pablo Casals

A famous Spanish musician, also noted for his humanitarian beliefs.

(1876 - 1973)

I'm Hip-hop, the rapping rabbit from a
starship far away,
It looks so good down here on Earth,
I think I'm going to stay.
I just love this planet and you human
beings too,
And I've bounced across five galaxies
to have a word with you...

LIFE EDUCATION

You're Special, Too

Written by
Alexandra Parsons

Illustrated by
Ann Johns, John Shackell, and Stuart Harrison

FRANKLIN WATTS
A Division of Grolier Publishing
LONDON • NEW YORK • HONG KONG • SYDNEY
DANBURY, CONNECTICUT

First American Edition 1997 by
Franklin Watts
A Division of Grolier Publishing
Sherman Turnpike
Danbury, Connecticut 06816

10 9 8 7 6 5 4 3 2 1

Library of Congress Cataloging-in-Publication
Data
Parsons, Alexandra.
    You're Special, Too / Alexandra Parsons.
  -- 1st American ed.
      p.   cm. --(Life education)
    Includes index.
    Summary: Introduces the concepts of
self-esteem, friendship and regard for others
and the environment.
    ISBN 0-531-14422-4
    1. Conduct of life--Juvenile literature.
  [1. Conduct of life.]
  I. Title. II. Series
  BJ1581.2.P364 1997
  241--dc20   96-16323
                                 CIP AC

Edited by: Helen Lanz
Designed by: Sally Boothroyd
Commissioned photography by:
Peter Millard
Illustrations by: Ann Johns,
John Shackell, and Stuart Harrison

Printed in Italy

Acknowledgments:
Commissioned photography by Peter Millard: 8,
10, 18, 19, 20, 25.
Researched photographs: Sally & Richard
Greenhill 15; Hutchinson Library 22 (bottom
three); Robert Harding 13, 22 (top left).
Artwork: all cartoons of "alien" by Stuart
Harrison. Other cartoon illustrations by Ann
Johns: cover, 6 (both); 14-15; 18; 20 (bottom); 23
(all): John Shackell: title page; contents page; 8-9;
11 (both); 12-13; 16-17; 19; (top); 17; 24-25.

Franklin Watts and Life Education International
are indebted to Vince Hatton and Laurie Noffs
for their invaluable help.

Franklin Watts would like to extend their special
thanks to all the actors who appear in the Life
Education books:

Calum Heath   Jade Hoffman
Frances Lander   Karamdeep Sandhar

Contents

Making a difference . . . .

Our world is wonderful because of the people in it! People like you and me and the person sitting next to you. Each one of us can make a huge difference. We can make a difference in the lives of our friends and our families, and a difference to our neighborhood and even our planet!

Here are some ways you can make a pleasant difference in someone's life:

You could help out a friend.

You could show people how much you love them.

You could do something to make your neighborhood a nicer place to be.

You could do something to help the people of the world who are frightened and hungry.

Thinking of others
is a nice thing to do.

These kids are sure
good examples for you.

You've got great power,
so use it with care.

Make someone's day
and show that you're fair.

What's kind, what's unkind

We humans can do good things but we also have the power to make people's lives unhappy. Why do that? There are many reasons. Some people get angry with themselves and take it out on other people. Some people get stressed out and just haven't got time for kind thoughts, and some people are just plain selfish and don't care about anyone except themselves.
It takes all sorts to make our world.

Let us hope you don't meet too many people like these:

Get out of my way carrot-head! Your head's on fire... no one's going to play with you.

Feelings can get hurt just like knees can get scraped, but hurt feelings are harder to heal. Do you think it's right to hurt people's feelings just because of the way they look? What kind of person do you think the bully is?

What an awful day! The boss has gone mad, the train broke down on the way home... Why aren't you in bed? I haven't got time to read to you! Go upstairs AT ONCE!

That wasn't very nice, was it? He's had a hard day, but that's no reason to take it out on someone else. (Just because your Mom or Dad shouts at you once in a while, it doesn't mean they don't love you!)

How selfish! Some people only see their own needs and never think about others. What kind of people do you think they're going to grow up to be?

Being selfish and mean, as you can see,

Hurts other people as quick as can be.

Why can't we all be thoughtful and kind?

Patient and sweet, keeping each other in mind?

Think about it! . . . .

Imagine sitting in front of a pile of presents and saying you don't want any of them because you don't like the color of the wrapping paper! Isn't that stupid? But some people go about their lives like that. They make up their minds before they know the facts. This is called prejudice.

So who's prejudiced?

Unfortunately for the world, a lot of people suffer from prejudice. They refuse to listen to other ideas, and they are frightened of difference and change. Try to imagine a world without differences. Imagine if all your friends were exactly the same, all their houses were exactly the same, and there was only one kind of food in the world because everyone wanted the same thing. The world would be a very dull place indeed.

You can't tell what's inside a package until you open it up. And you can't tell what people are like until you make an effort to get to know them.

What a boring bunch you are!

I'm a hip-hopping rabbit,
but I'm pretty smart –

I know how people get in
trouble from the start.

They make up their minds
without knowing what's true

So just be careful – don't
let that happen to you.

Why do you think some groups of
people all want to look the same?

Differences can be fun!

We all come from different families and we have experiences of life that no one else has had. That is what makes us all so interesting. It is fun to find out about other people, other families, and other ways of doing things.

That's better!

Story of a friendship . . .

This is a story about two good friends, Eddie and Billy.

Can you come over to my house tonight? Mom said she'd get pizza.

That's great.

I'll invent some more ghost stories to scare yooouuuu...

Your stories are so silly. They make me laugh till my tummy aches!

They look fun, Andy. Let's see if we can play with them tomorrow.

Good idea, Clare.

Silly Billy's blind!

Eddie thinks he's a guide dog. Woof woof!

All blind people are a real burden, poor things. They can't help it, but if you have anything to do with them, you just end up taking care of them the whole time. I don't want you playing with Billy. And that Eddie, he must think he's some sort of guide dog!

Those awful children have been upsetting you again. Just wait until I talk to their parents.

No, Mom! You're so embarrassing! They don't bother me. But I wish they wouldn't pick on Eddie. I'm blind and that's it, but they shouldn't pick on Eddie just because he's my friend.

If you don't want to be my friend anymore, I'd sort of understand.

I'm not going to let those miserable bullies tell me who to be friends with.

Clare and Andy's first reaction was to play with Billy and Eddie. They saw two happy kids walking down the street and they wanted to join in. But when their mom said something untrue and hurtful about blind people, Clare and Andy saw Silly Billy and a guide dog, and they felt it was OK to be rude and unkind to them. That's what prejudice can do. Dangerous, isn't it?

Everyone is different in some way — whether you are tall or short, deaf or blind. Real friends like people for WHO they are.

Who would think
it can ever be right,

To be mean and nasty —
it's not very bright.

Stirring up hate and
calling people names,

That's not for us, those
are stupid people's games.

What's good, what's bad?

Very few people are all good or all bad. People are not that simple, and life isn't that simple. Good people sometimes make mistakes, and people who are just plain nasty can have their good days. But mostly, people who do bad things either don't think about how other people are going to feel, or else they don't care one way or another.

Treating others as you want to be treated

Oh, no! Someone's stolen all the children's Christmas presents from under the tree!

What's happened? When I left we had a pile of Christmas presents under the tree. What kind of evil-minded so-and-so would steal presents...?

... and on Christmas Eve too.

Ahem, ahem, excuse me!

Who are you?

I'm your conscience.

My what?

I'm supposed to remind you about right and wrong.

Wrong? I'll tell you what's wrong, somebody stealing my Christmas presents, that's what's wrong. Stop dripping tinsel over my carpet and go annoy him.

Well, I thought I'd start with you.

Why me?

Because you've stolen Christmas presents yourself.

Shut up, will you! I feel really terrible.

Maybe if you took those presents back, you'd feel a lot better.

Will you stop trying to make me feel bad about stealing? You'll put me out of business! I am a burglar, after all!

Well, how do you like it when someone steals from you?

I don't like it one little bit, not one bit. Now buzz off, before I nail you to the top of the tree.

I can't get through to him. He knows having things stolen makes HIM miserable, but he doesn't care about making others miserable. Being his conscience is like talking to a brick wall. And he's SO rude to me. I'm applying for a transfer.

When you do something bad, and it doesn't feel right,

You've gotta sort it out so you can sleep at night.

Listen to the little voice inside your head,

Think how you'd feel if it were YOU instead.

17

That's mine! . . . .

Do you think it is OK to take something or borrow something without asking? Maybe you should ask the people who had something taken how they feel about it.

Mothers' Day This is a story about Ben and a bunch of flower

What did you get your mom for Mothers' Day, Ben?

Oh, no! I forgot!

These will make Mom happy, they're her favorite flowers.

Oh, darling, they're beautiful! Where did you get them?

Well, um, I...

Pesky kids! I'll never get the Park Keeper of the Year Award now!

I'm sorry, Mr. Park Keeper. I just didn't think...

That's OK, just remember that the flowers in the park are for everyone's enjoyment. It was good of you to come and own up. Here, take these for your mom.

The "disappearing" ruler

This is a story about Lucy, who thought only of herself.

Oh, no! I forgot my ruler. Ms. Jones will get really angry with me.

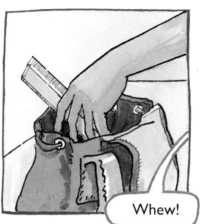

Whew!

Now I told you all yesterday to be sure to remember your rulers because today we are going to learn about measuring. What's the matter, Sanjay?

I don't know, Ms. Jones. I know I brought my ruler. It was in my bag this morning, but now it's just disappeared!

Rulers don't disappear, Sanjay. Careless children forget to bring them to school and then they think they can come up with unbelievable tales of disappearing rulers! Stay behind after school.

Taking things from others is never, ever cool.

All of us should obey that simple rule.

And just because you need it, it still isn't right –

Don't take from others – be honest and upright.

19

Telling fibs . . . .

If people thought it was all right to tell lies,
life would be very confusing and very unfair.
So it is always important to tell the truth.

Coward's lies

Well, he may get
away with breaking
the window, but he's
lost his best friend.
Was it worth it?

Mean and nasty lies

Sooner or later Jenny and Mary are going to work
out just who has been saying what to whom.

Great Aunt Edna's awful hat

This is a story about how Emily learned the meaning of the word "tact."

Mom, you and Dad will be coming to the school play, won't you? I have to know by tomorrow.

I'm so looking forward to your play, dear. What do you think of my hat?

YOU CAN'T POSSIBLY...

Come here, Emily. I want to talk to you.

Aunt Edna bought that hat especially for today. She's so proud of it — you can't be unkind.

Mom, I'll die of embarrassment if my friends see her in that... birds' nest! She asked what I think of it, and I'm going to tell her! You're always telling me to tell the truth.

Not in this case, darling. Try to think of her feelings. Your friends have probably got aunts with hats too. I'm sure they'll understand.

Er... I was just going to say you can't possibly... see how... er... interesting it looks from the back!

If you want to be a person who's good and kind,

Never tell lies that land others in a bind.

But keeping to yourself what you think of aunty's hat,

Well, that's just the work of a diplomat!

That's called being tactful, darling. Well done!

Do this! Do that! . . . . .

Why won't grown-ups ever stop telling you what to do? Think of all the things you have to do during the day, and why you are told to do them. Why do you have to brush your teeth? Why do you have to go school? Why aren't you allowed to watch television all night? Even when you grow up, people will still tell you what to do. Don't walk on the grass! No parking! Don't drop litter! Why are there so many rules????

Reasons for rules

People expect certain things from life. Children have a right to expect love and help from their parents. Sometimes that means nagging you to brush your teeth so you don't get a cavity, or hauling you off to bed on time so you aren't tired and cranky at school.

We all have a right to an education; that's why we have schools. We have a right to cross the road without being killed, so there are rules of the road. We have a right to keep the things we own, so there are laws against stealing. You have to have rules (not too many, not too few) to protect people's rights.

Too many rules

Sorry, madam, you can't buy tomatoes or peas except on Wednesdays. I'll have to confiscate them.

I'm arresting you for not wearing a hat when the temperature is below 55°F.

Is that a fur collar I see? They were outlawed under section 8 of law 476/9ZXP only last week.

You'll be in prison for a long time, sir. Your windscreen is dirty, your dog doesn't have his seat belt on, and you failed to empty your fuel tank before you entered the turn.

Is that a book I see in your pocket, sir? Private ownership of books is banned, sir. This is a most serious offense. I shall have to ask you to accompany me to the station, sir.

No rules at all

Nobody wants to be told what to do,

But with no rules, the world would be a zoo!

If you stop to think why the rules are there,

You'll see it's to make sure that all is fair.

You are not safe in the streets, not safe in your own home. Everybody is supposed to do what they want, but nobody does anything anymore. It's chaos.

If I ruled the world . . . . .

How would you organize a perfect world? And how would you stop people from spoiling it? Our world certainly isn't perfect. For instance, you've got greedy, selfish people who think the rules do not apply to them. But you also have wonderful, hardworking people who really are making a difference to people's lives. How can you help make the world a finer place for everyone?

I just want you to know, kids, that I really appreciate every little drop of thoughtfulness. Every kind act makes life better somewhere for someone.

Well, it's my turn to rule the world now. I just think everyone should have everything they want.

It's not so simple, Your Majesty. Some people have nothing and others have everything. Some people want everything and some people want very little. It's hard work sorting everything out – no one's been able to do it yet.

Well, now it's my turn. My solution is... that someone should invent a magic dust to sprinkle over all the bad, selfish people, so everyone is nice.

Impossible to do, if you don't mind my saying so, Your Majesty. One, there is no suc dust; two, if there were, how much would it cost and who would pay for it; three, has anyone thought about side effects?

My solution is this. If everyone made a little difference, in their family, in their school, in their neighborhood, one day all the good patches would kind of meet up!

An excellent suggestion, Your Majesty. Now perhaps you could start the ball rolling by getting to bed on time without making a fuss!

You need a loving framework to build society.

To make the world a better place, fit for you and me,

We must respect all people's rights; we're equal every one.

Be kind to one other, kids. My rapping rhymes are done.

LETTER FROM LIFE EDUCATION

Dear Friends:

The first Life Education Center was opened in Sydney, Australia, in 1979. Founded by the Rev. Ted Noffs, the Life Education program came about as a result of his many years of work with drug addicts and their families. Noffs realized that preventive education, beginning with children from the earliest possible age all the way into their teenage years, was the only long-term solution to drug abuse and other related social problems.

Life Education pioneered the use of technology in a "Classroom of the 21st Century," designed to show how drugs, including nicotine and alcohol, can destroy the delicate balance of human life. In every Life Education classroom, electronic displays show the major body systems, including the respiratory, nervous, digestive and immune systems. There is also a talking brain, a wondrous star ceiling, and Harold the Giraffe, Life Education's official mascot. Programs start in preschool and continue through high school.

Life Education also conducts parents' programs including violence prevention classes, and it has also begun to create interactive software for home and school computers.

There are Life Education Centers operating in seven countries (Thailand, the United States, the United Kingdom, New Zealand, Australia, Hong Kong, and New Guinea), and there is a Life Education home page on the Internet (the address is http://www.lec.org/).

If you would like to learn more about Life Education International contact us at one of the addresses listed below or, if you have a computer with a modem, you can write to Harold the Giraffe at Harold@lec.org and you'll find out that a giraffe can send E-mail!

Let's learn to live.

All of us at the Life Education Center.

Life Education, USA
149 Addison Ave
Elmhurst, Illinois
60126
USA
Tel: 630 530 8999
Fax: 630 530 7241

Life Education, UK
20 Long Lane
London
EC1A 9HL
United Kingdom
Tel: 0171 600 6969
Fax: 0171 600 6979

Life Education, Australia
PO Box 1671
Potts Point
NSW 2011
Australia
Tel: 0061 2 358 2466
Fax: 0061 2 357 2569

Life Education, New Zealand
126 The Terrace
PO Box 10-769
Wellington
New Zealand
Tel: 0064 4 472 9620
Fax: 0064 4 472 9609

Useful words

Bully Someone who picks on, threatens, or hurts other children. Bullies often don't feel very good about themselves, and they want other people to feel worse than they do.

Conscience The part of you that decides if something is right or wrong. For example, sometimes you may be tempted to tell a lie to get out of trouble, but your conscience will tell you this is wrong.

Neighborhood Your local area, including all the streets and houses and the people living in them, along with the local parks, sports centers, and so on.

People's rights Your rights are all the things the law says you should have: for example, a home, food, and education. You also have a right to be safe from robbers or from careless drivers in the street.

Prejudice Judging people by how they look, before giving them a chance to show you how they really are.

Tact Thinking of other people's feelings and, where possible, avoiding saying things you know will hurt them.

Index

Useful addresses

Character Education Institute
8918 Tesoro Drive, Suite 575
San Antonio, TX 78217
Telephone: 210-829-1727
Toll-free: 800-284-0499
Fax: 210-829-1729

Junior Optimist Clubs
4494 Lindell Boulevard
St. Louis, MO 63108
Telephone: 314-371-6000
Fax: 314-371-6006

Key Club International
3636 Woodview Trace
Indianapolis, IN 46268
Telephone: 317-875-8755

Quest International
P.O. Box 566
Granville, OH 43023
Telephone: 614-522-6400
Toll-free: 800-446-2700
Fax: 614-522-6580

U.S. Junior Chamber of
Commerce
P.O. Box 7
4 West 21st Street
Tulsa, OK 74102
Telephone: 918-584-2481
Fax: 918-582-7736

Youth Service America
1101 15th Street W., Suite 200
Washington, DC 20004
Telephone: 202-296-2992